COUNTRIES ON THE WORLD STAGE

SPOTLIGHT ON The United Kingdom

Tracy Sue Walker

Lerner Publications ◆ Minneapolis

Content consultant: Dr. Keith Pluymers, Illinois State University

Lerner Publications Company
An imprint of Lerner Publishing Group, Inc.
241 First Avenue North
Minneapolis, MN 55401 USA

For reading levels and more information, look up this title at www.lernerbooks.com.

Main body text set in Aptifer Sans LT Pro Semibold.
Typeface provided by Linotype AG.

Illustration on page 13 by Laura K. Westlund.

Designer: Athena Currier

Library of Congress Cataloging-in-Publication Data

Names: Walker, Tracy Sue, author.
Title: Spotlight on the United Kingdom / Tracy Sue Walker.
Description: Minneapolis : Lerner Publications , [2024] | Series: Countries on the World stage | Includes bibliographical references and index. | Audience: Ages 8–12 | Audience: Grades 4–6 | Summary: "The United Kingdom has a rich history. Learn about the UK's early history and how it grew to become a world superpower. Discover how a land once ruled by monarchs navigates the modern political landscape"— Provided by publisher.
Identifiers: LCCN 2022046758 (print) | LCCN 2022046759 (ebook) | ISBN 9781728492032 (library binding) | ISBN 9798765602591 (paperback) | ISBN 9781728496740 (ebook)
Subjects: LCSH: Great Britain—Juvenile literature. | Northern Ireland—Juvenile literature.
Classification: LCC DA27.5 .W345 2024 (print) | LCC DA27.5 (ebook) | DDC 941—dc23/eng/20220927

LC record available at https://lccn.loc.gov/2022046758
LC ebook record available at https://lccn.loc.gov/2022046759

Manufactured in the United States of America
1-53142-51152-2/21/2023

TABLE OF CONTENTS

INTRODUCTION

End of an Era

ON SEPTEMBER 8, 2022, AN OFFICIAL NOTICE WAS POSTED ON THE GATES OF BUCKINGHAM PALACE IN LONDON, ENGLAND.

The note said that Queen Elizabeth II had died. She served as queen of the United Kingdom for seventy years. Queen Elizabeth II was the only monarch most UK citizens had ever known. People left flowers and teddy bears outside the palace. Many people waited for hours to say goodbye

Flowers, cards, and other items left outside Buckingham Palace to honor Queen Elizabeth II

to their queen. The monarchy had been in the UK for over a thousand years. People wondered what would happen to the monarchy after the queen's death.

CHAPTER 1

The Start of the UK

People first came to the land that is now the UK sometime between eight hundred thousand and one million years ago. Archaeologists have found some of their tools and art. Then Celtic people arrived in the area in 1000 BCE. When the Romans invaded in 43 CE, it brought a blending of peoples and cultures. And with the Romans came the introduction of Christianity. By the fifth century, Angles and Saxons from Germanic-speaking Europe invaded and formed many smaller kingdoms. This created

A statue of William the Conqueror in his birthplace of Falaise, France

a further mixture of cultures in Britain. Then, in 1066 CE, William the Conqueror united the kingdoms and ruled them as a monarch.

UNITING THE KINGDOM

From the 1100s to 1801, the relationship between England, Ireland, Scotland, and Wales was unpredictable. In 1543 England and Wales officially unified. Queen Elizabeth I of England had no children. So, when she died in 1603, her cousin King James VI of Scotland was crowned. He became King James I of England and Ireland as well. He gave himself the title King of Great Britain and tried to unite the countries. However, it wasn't until 1707 that England (including Wales) and Scotland officially united into the Kingdom of Great Britain. Ireland had been linked to England since 1172 but officially joined in an Act of Union In 1801. From this time on, the United Kingdom of Great Britain and Ireland was formed. The Union Jack flag reflects this union. In 1921 Northern Ireland was created when the rest of Ireland seceded from the UK.

King James I ruled England from 1603 to 1625.

For hundreds of years, rule passed from one monarch to another, and Roman Catholicism spread throughout Britain by monks and missionaries. Fights sometimes broke out when power changed hands. The Tudor period (1485–1603) started when King Henry VIII broke from the Catholic Church because it did not allow divorce. He formed the Church of England in 1534. Later, King Henry's daughter Queen Elizabeth I rose to power. Serving from 1558 to 1603, she was a popular monarch and made the country rich.

The time Queen Elizabeth I ruled England is called the Elizabethan Age.

In 1607 British colonists created a settlement called Jamestown. It is located in modern Jamestown, Virginia, in the United States.

Britain also wanted to control lands outside its borders. In the 1500s, it started taking over lands that Indigenous peoples lived on. This process is called colonization. The British often attacked Indigenous peoples. Many Indigenous peoples stood up and fought back. Over many years, the British Empire colonized lands that are now part of North America, Australia, New Zealand, Asia, Africa, and Central and South America. The British Empire took resources from Indigenous peoples so that the British could become wealthier and more powerful.

Britain was also part of the transatlantic slave trade, which kidnapped people from Africa and forced them into slavery in the Americas. From 1640 to 1807, it is estimated that Britain kidnapped 3.1 million people from Africa. Britain ended slavery within its borders in 1838. But it helped make a process that spread slavery in the Americas.

The monarchy became less powerful during Queen Victoria's reign from 1837 to 1901. The monarchy shifted from ruling the nation into a more ceremonial role. Many people respect the monarchy, and members of the monarchy often meet with world leaders. After Queen Victoria's reign, poverty rose and living conditions worsened.

Then World War I (1914–1918) broke out. The UK fought alongside Serbia, the Soviet Union (a former country that included Russia and fourteen other republics), France, Italy, and the United States, and together they made up the Allies. They fought against Germany, Austria-Hungary, Bulgaria, and the Ottoman Empire. The Allies won the war, but two decades later, the countries would be fighting another world war.

CHAPTER 2

Rolling Hills and Royalty

The UK is a country in the British Isles off the northwest coast of Europe. Four nations—England, Wales, Scotland, and Northern Ireland—make up the UK. England, Wales, and Scotland are located on the island of Great Britain. Northern Ireland sits across the Irish Sea and shares a land border with the independent country of Ireland.

to more islands of Scotland
ATLANTIC OCEAN
NORTH SEA
N
SCOTLAND
Edinburgh
Belfast
NORTHERN IRELAND
REPUBLIC OF IRELAND (ÊIRE)
Miles
0 25 50 75 100
0 50 100 150
Kilometers
WALES
ENGLAND
Cardiff
London
CELTIC SEA
English Channel
BELGIUM
FRANCE
ARCTIC OCEAN
NORTH AMERICA
UNITED KINGDOM
EUROPE
ASIA
ATLANTIC OCEAN
AFRICA
PACIFIC OCEAN
SOUTH AMERICA
PACIFIC OCEAN
INDIAN OCEAN
AUSTRALIA
SOUTHERN OCEAN
UK capital
Country capital
International border
Mountains

The Urquhart Castle sits on the rolling hills next to Loch Ness in Scotland.

During the last ice age, thick sheets of ice called glaciers covered the lands that are now the UK. These glaciers carved valleys and created many narrow and deep lakes called lochs. The southern UK is covered with rolling, green hills.

The UK is growing increasingly diverse. People have immigrated to the UK from many places including India, Pakistan, Poland, Romania, the Caribbean, and Germany. These cultures enrich the UK and are reflected in the varieties of food, music, and art found in the country.

People walk past stores in Cardiff, Wales.

CHAPTER 3

A Changing Economy

The British Empire was the largest empire the world has ever known, and much of its economy was built off colonization. But after World War I, the country's economy was in trouble. Within the empire, many countries were fighting for their independence. The UK tried to repair the harm it had caused the colonies as well as strengthen its own country. In 1926 the UK created an organization called the Commonwealth of Nations. The UK promised that all nations in the Commonwealth would be treated as equals.

Representatives of several countries attended the 1926 Imperial Conference and created the Commonwealth of Nations.

Farmers pick strawberries in a greenhouse.

Throughout its history, agriculture has played an important role in the UK. Over 70 percent of its land is currently used for agriculture. Most of the land used to grow crops is in southeastern England. The temperatures and rainfall in this area help crops grow. Almost 80 percent of the land in Scotland is used for grazing and agriculture. Mining is another historically important industry in the UK. Coal is the most significant mineral that is mined today. However, the UK is also known for mining limestone, tin, iron ore, lead, and clay.

World War II (1939–1945) started when Adolf Hitler and Nazi Germany invaded Poland. The Nazis used people's anger over the economy to spread hatred about people who were different from them. The Nazis mainly targeted Jewish people, but they also harmed Roma people, gay people, and people with disabilities. The UK was one of the countries that made up the World War II Allies, which also included France, the United States, and the Soviet Union. The Allies fought Germany, Italy, and Japan. The Allies won, but the British economy was hurt after the war. Many cities in the UK suffered damage from enemy bombing. Because of this, the UK owed a lot of money to other countries.

London after being bombed by Germany sometime between September 1940 and May 1941

In the years following World War II, the country rebuilt and created a national health-care system for all of its citizens. The UK left some of the countries it had colonized as well. One of these was India, which the UK had ruled for almost ninety years.

The UK economy also shifted from being more agricultural and industrial toward services. The service industry still makes up the largest part of the British economy. London is one of the world's leading financial hubs. Financial services include real estate, banking, insurance, and investment companies. Tourism is one of the UK's most important service industries. The country is the sixth-largest tourist destination in the world. The UK tourism industry was negatively impacted by the COVID-19 pandemic.

The modern UK has a free market economy. Buyers and sellers of goods and services can buy and sell without much involvement from the government. The UK trades most of its goods with countries in the European Union (EU). The EU brings together a group of countries in Europe and helps its members with trade, security, and other issues. In 2019 more than 40 percent of all British goods and services were exported to the EU. The UK was a member of the European Union until January 2020, when a 2016 vote to leave the EU took effect. This decision is known as Brexit.

EXPLORE BREXIT

Brexit combines the words Britain and *exit*. Some citizens felt that leaving the EU would give the UK more control over such things as the economy and immigration. Others felt it would hurt the UK's economy, which relied on trading with such EU countries as Germany, France, and the Netherlands.

Members of Parliament meet in the House of Commons in 2020.

CHAPTER 4

Crown, Cabinet, and Council

In modern times, the United Kingdom has a constitutional monarchy with a parliamentary government. This means decisions about lawmaking and budgets are made by members of the UK Parliament.

The prime minister is the leader of the national government. The prime minister appoints members of the cabinet. This team of twenty people leads departments that include national defense, health care, and foreign affairs. The prime

The House of Commons helps create laws. It is part of Parliament.

minister also oversees Parliament, which includes the House of Commons and the House of Lords. Together these houses work to pass new laws and make other national decisions. The 650

Members of Parliament debate a bill in the House of Lords.

members of the House of Commons are elected by the British people. However, the monarch appoints members of the House of Lords based on the prime minister's suggestions. Some people without a political party are chosen by the independent House of Lords Appointments Commission.

PARLIAMENTS AND ASSEMBLIES

The Parliament of the United Kingdom makes sure the government and councils represent the interests of all citizens across the UK. There is also a Welsh Parliament, a Scottish Parliament, and the Northern Ireland Assembly. These legislative bodies can pass laws that are specific to their individual countries.

Parliament is separate from local government councils. Councils are responsible for important services. Voters in counties, districts, and boroughs elect members of their local government. Members of these councils oversee fire and public safety departments, libraries, waste management, and transportation.

Election workers count ballots in Barry, Wales.

CONCLUSION

Looking Forward

RISHI SUNAK BECAME THE UK'S PRIME MINISTER IN OCTOBER 2022. He is the first person of color to lead the country. Many people hope he will help the country through its economic problems. Before becoming prime minister, Sunak met with King Charles III. Charles became monarch a month earlier after the passing of his mother, Queen Elizabeth II.

Some of the Commonwealth nations, which were made part of the British Empire against their will, want to leave the colonial past behind. They are considering leaving the Commonwealth to become republics. Barbados removed the British monarch as its head of state and became a republic in 2021.

Many people wonder what the future of the UK will look like. The decisions the country makes now will impact both the UK and the world.

Rishi Sunak gives his first speech as prime minister on October 25, 2022.

TIMELINE

About 1,000,000–800,000 BCE	The earliest known humans arrive in areas that are now the United Kingdom.
43 CE	Romans invade Celtic Britain.
1543 CE	Wales and England join to become one country.
1601–1997	The British Empire is a powerful system around the world and is controlled by England.
1603	James VI of Scotland becomes James I of England and Ireland. He combines the nations as Great Britain.
1914–1918	The UK fights in World War I. The country and its allies win the war.
1921	Northern Ireland joins the UK.
1939–1945	The UK fights in World War II alongside the other Allies. The Allies win the war.
2021	Barbados, which had been part of the Commonwealth, becomes a republic.
2022	Rishi Sunak becomes prime minister.

UNITED KINGDOM FAST FACTS

Official name: United Kingdom of Great Britain and Northern Ireland

UK population: 65,105,246

Land area: 94,058 square miles (243,609 sq. km)

Largest city: London

Capital city: London

Form of Government: constitutional monarchy with parliamentary government

Official language: English

Flag:

GLOSSARY

agriculture: the production of crops and raising of livestock

appoint: to choose someone to have a particular job

culture: the beliefs, practices, and characteristics of a certain society or group

economy: the process or system by which goods and services are made, sold, and bought in a country

empire: a group of countries or regions that are controlled by one ruler or government

European Union: an economic and political union between twenty-seven European countries formed to bring together the countries of Europe. It helps its member countries with issues such as trade and security.

export: something that is sent to another country to be sold

immigration: the process of people moving from one country to another

monarchy: a form of government in which a country is ruled by a monarch who has total control, such as a king or a queen

parliament: the group of people who make the laws in some forms of government

LEARN MORE

Anthony, William. *Visit to England*. Minneapolis: Bearport, 2023.

Britannica Kids: Northern Ireland
https://kids.britannica.com/kids/article/Northern-Ireland/353299

Britannica Kids: Scotland
https://kids.britannica.com/kids/article/Scotland/346211

Davies, Monika. *England*. Minneapolis: Bellwether Media, 2023.

Kiddle: Wales Facts for Kids
https://kids.kiddle.co/Wales

Mooney, Carla. *United Kingdom*. Minneapolis: Abdo, 2023.

National Geographic Kids: United Kingdom
https://kids.nationalgeographic.com/geography/countries/article/united-kingdom

Walker, Tracy Sue. *Spotlight on the United States*. Minneapolis: Lerner Publications, 2024.

INDEX

PHOTO ACKNOWLEDGMENTS

Image credits:, Richard Maidment/Shutterstock, p. 5; Pack-Shot/Shutterstock, p. 7; Wikimedia Commons PD, p. 8; Photos.com/Getty Images, p. 9; mikroman6/Getty Images, p. 10; Juan Vte. Muñoz/Getty Images, p. 14; Maremagnum/Getty Images, p. 15; Chronicle/Alamy Stock Photo, p. 17; Kelvin Murray/Getty Images, p. 18; Everett Collection/Shutterstock, p. 19; House of Commons - PA Images/Getty Images, p. 21; Nuwan/Getty Images, p. 23; KIRSTY WIGGLESWORTH/Getty Images, p. 24; ComposedPix/Shutterstock, p. 25; Bloomberg/Getty Images, p. 27; Igillustrator/Shutterstock, p. 29.

Cover: Andy Shiels/Shutterstock.